Table of Contents

Note to Parents and Teachers

The Wonder Readers Next Steps: Social Studies series supports national standards related to social studies. These titles use text structures that support early readers, specifically with a close photo/text match, glossary, and words to know. Each book is perfectly leveled to support the reader at the right reading level, and the topics are of high interest. Early readers will gain success when they are presented with a book that is of interest to them and is written at the appropriate level.

On the Job

Firefighters are very busy
at the fire station.

They check the fire trucks.

They check the hoses.

They check fire **hydrants**.

Equipment

Firefighters hurry when the fire **alarm** rings.

They wear heavy gear
to **protect** them from fire.

They drive fire engines
to the fire.

They use hoses to spray
water on the fire.

Helping People

Firefighters search for people who are trapped.

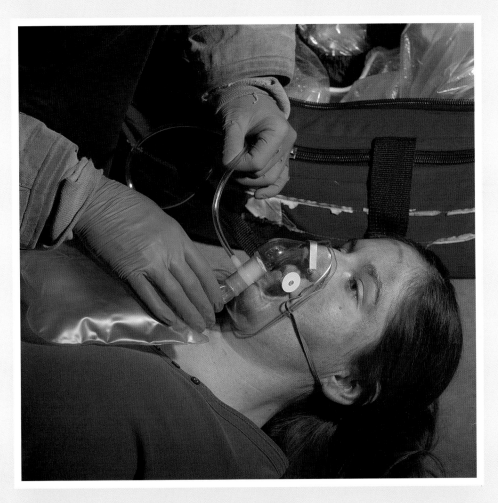

They help people
who are hurt.

They **rescue** people
who are trapped.

They check smoke alarms in homes.

Fire Safety

They teach children
about fire safety.

They tell children what
to do in case of a fire.

We are proud of
our firefighters!

Now Try This!

Write a thank you card to send to your local fire station. You can decorate your card with illustrations from this book. You could also write a thank you note about a firefighting activity. For example, you could write "Thank you for teaching me about fire safety." Mail your thank you card to your local fire station.

Glossary

alarm	a device with a bell, buzzer, or siren that warns people of danger
hydrant	a large, upright pipe with a valve that draws water from the city's water supply; hydrants supply water for fighting fires.
protect	to guard or keep safe from harm
rescue	to save someone who is in danger

Internet Sites

FactHound offers a safe, fun way to find Internet sites related to this book. All of the sites on FactHound have been researched by our staff.

Here's all you do:

Visit *www.facthound.com*

Type in this code: 9781476523620

 Check out projects, games and lots more at **www.capstonekids.com**

Index